D1572319

THE LADY FROM THE DARK GREEN HILLS

THE LADY FROM
THE DARK GREEN HILLS poems by
Jim Hall

Three   Rivers   Press

Pittsburgh

ACKNOWLEDGMENTS

Acknowledgement is gratefully made to
editors of the following magazines in
which some of these poems first appeared:

*Antioch Review, Epoch, Florida Quarterly,
Kansas Quarterly, Southern Poetry Review,
Three Rivers Poetry Journal, and
Wormwood Review.*
"The Lady from the Dark Green Hills,"
Copyright © 1968 by the Antioch Press.
First published in *The Antioch Review*,
Vol. 28, No. 4; reprinted by permission
of the editors.

*The publication of this book is supported
by a grant from the National Endowment for
the Arts in Washington, D.C., a Federal
agency.*

Library of Congress Catalog Card Number: 75-34584
ISBN 0-915606-00-3
Copyright © 1976 by Three Rivers Press
Printed and bound in the United States of America

CONTENTS

III. The Lady From the Dark Green Hills

I DECOMPOSING WOMEN

DECOMPOSING WOMEN

Decomposing women
can be found in vacant lots
in the deep underbrush

They are not always sexually
molested but their clothes
are usually disarranged
and dented beer cans can be
found in the vicinity

They vanish from shopping
malls where they were buying rock
records or panty hose and
their car is still sitting
in the empty lot next morning

Most often
there is the slightest sign
of struggle in the car, maybe
a drop of blood on the steering
wheel, some long hair snagged
on the door

Many times
there is even a single red
shoe left behind on
the floorboard like a note
dashed off in the dark

MARTHA'S DAUGHTERS

Her daughters are bald and water
Awes their eyes. They crawl in
Their bedroom and gnaw on cubes
Of ice. Martha, their only Mother,
Watches from the small door.

Something is wrong. Awful
Light shines through their
Skin like a slow dawn from
Within. They are old enough
To date, but no one calls. They
Do not walk, and thick heads
Of hair grow like shawls from their
Shoulders. A doctor saw them once
And put his black hand on Martha's
Cheek. Said nothing.

She locks the door. They caw
And beat the dark rug. In the hall
She draws a calm circle in the dust
On a table and feels a splitting yawn
Bloom. They bomb the door with hands
Like flowers. Like mudcoated flowers.
The yawn, a howl, fills her as their
Voices cauterize the dark air. Their
Mudgloved fists thicken on the door.

Preacher Hall honks outside. The awful
Door growls beside her Bible. And her
Yawn empties into the evening air.

THE PRESIDENT OF THE WORLD'S LARGEST BIBLE COLLEGE, AFTER HAVING AN AFFAIR WITH A STUDENT, RESIGNS

So long
you must have known
        they'd come for you
        as they do in the Testament
        with large skull-crashing stones
that this drove you on with her. A tennis
court meeting:

        she had legs striped with muscles
        and hair like the wind and a forehand
better than yours.

Not temptation. At last, a commandment-
        THOU SHALT FALL IN LOVE, court certain
        disaster.
        Take her to a beach motel and let her teach
you those strokes you thought only pros could have.

Here they come
        through the fading pillow case with pock-
        marked stones to ease your guilt
        and still your flesh in a rocketing moment
        of unison.

Her net game needed work
    her overhead was rusty
So you beat those balls between you
    till they were dead and light as touch.

And then they were in the room piling
    rocks around the bucking bed
    going out for more.

The game is over.
    You both leap the net and embrace
    above it, floating like lobs.
    And you see they've piled the rocks
    below you
So you can climb back to Earth.

HOOK EM HORNS

Her hair ricochets beneath her cowgirl hat
and her compressed pom pom breasts
make the sun blaze over deserted
shopping malls and addicts
us to her methadone movements.

The way she cocks
her head and kicks her skirt up a glimpse
and jabs both bullheaded fists at the crowd
is what makes dockworkers
glide warm into bars and mumble.

Her knotted bottom, trained to perk
is what grinds the salt from soldiers' tears
and brings them back
from the sleek bellies of unamerican women.

It's her wisp waist, blunt legs, gold
dusted arms. It's the razor line
between hip and knee where the thigh hair
stops
that sells Chevrolets
surges the Dow
and inexplicably soothes the narrow Italian
loading his oily blue magnum.

One thing more, only: her eyes.
Iced tea, blood slush.
They suck us round her curves

and we are hooked and raised on them
and on her steel smile
her fast breath
her megaphonic basso.
The horns curl out of
thick skulls throughout America.
We see red
and rush.
At first,
there's nothing there.

THE STORM

Now that it's no more than a persistent
trickling,
I know how it must have been to be
The Phantom of the Opera. To have
the muffled orchestration
punctuated by thunderous applause,
tremble through the opera floor,
the empty dressing rooms,
then through my stone slab sewer cave.
To have the houselights
dim my own bulb so low the moth flies away.

I know how it must have been to have my Mrs. Phantom
be a sewer socialite, an opera addict.
Arriving and exiting through a ladies' room stall.
Leaving me to thrash alone
through the bombast of Beethoven,
grabbing my pillow
clutching sanity's little finger.

Until the opera ends.
The audience stands twice, pauses and leaves.
Their carriages clicking across my patio roof,
and the gasp of commodes above my bedroom,
where men in tails,
as famous, popular and handsome as Christ
change champagne to piss.
Filling my riverbed
and my wife's shoes
as she hikes home to me, recharged.

If they were pretty
or opened the door wide enough,
he would unlatch his raincoat and let
it spring out.
His eyes pleading
as if he were a beggar and this a withered hand.

Five said, "Jesus Christ!"
Most shrieked and bolted.
One laughed.
One cried.
And the last one invited him inside.

When the officers arrived
he mewled and denied it all.
They took him in.
The star witnesses assembled
but since no one had noticed his face
they were all forced to study
five dangling suspects.

Still there was no positive identification
Certainly nothing that could stand up in court.

THE CRAFT LADY

In the craft
shop she taught
us to braid her
hair into lanyards,
to shape her eyes
into almond plaques,
stained mahogany to
celebrate her tan thighs

       She moved about
us spreading
a word we could smell
but not pronounce in
long woodburning moments

       Short shorts
white as our eyes as
she bent to steady
a hand

       "Be careful,
you can't erase," she'd say,
while we burned
our slow platitudes into slabs
of her flesh

PREMATURE BURIAL

My mother tamps the earth
above this socket of soil.
Packing me for a long ride.
Pressing the blanket of
breathless black air tight
across my chest. A smothered
word works through. Is it
love? Or the crush of her body
creaking the bed.

She's going away now. I feel
her feet, their slight depressions
across my forehead, like kisses
goodnight. I begin to move.
First, only working a finger free,
then swiveling the wrist, loosening.

The night wrestles me to the bed.

And now, the light tears my eyes,
she's back! Brushing the dust off
my face, picking crumbs of dirt
from my clenched eye corners.
She whispers the word again.
It is *love.* She seems not to
care that I've clawed out
of another night.

CUM LAUDE

She comes to me in new colors
in the crush of light that
bites white here in the offices
and flares up the sandspur sores
on her cheeks. Those unchecked pillows
of flesh, laps of stretch yellow pants,
forcing the double-knit weave to open up.
Darla, with black hair thick as flies,
and snaggled like old acrylic, is my
best student.

We love across my desk in conference
as she sucks in straws of breath-
a whistle in reverse. It is a rehearsal
for love she's never had, won't ever
have with a clean smooth man like me.

We go at it. My denims and natural
cottons and her pink red, thick red
blouse, all napped and spider webbed
with dying fabric. On either side
of an issue we make our eldritch love.
I autograph her mind. She stitches me
with choked off respect.

She gives in at last
to my views. She grunts a garish smile.

I whisper into print this note for you

Darla, when you leave.
When you find the rare book in which this
is hidden, don't trust me, not even now.
To me you are a bucket
I pour all this into.
Darla, bring this as a ticket.
Put on your snaggled argyles, your rubber
sandals, your crimson acrylic blouse and come.
I have your A. Your A, Darla. All of them.

ALICE AND THE BEASTS

Captured in a brief nap beneath the parasol of a
windy afternoon flower,
tiny Alice was quickly raped by a frog
who left her like a bean bag with a leak,
and hobbled off, a gasping old man.

Now, if Alice had been a good lay
or if the frog had been a visiting ambassador,
no account would be made of such strange matters.
But Alice was young,
in fact, only a calico puppy of a girl.
And the frog
was a horney toad that lurched on lily pads
all day dreaming amid the glaze
of just such damp delicious thighs as Alice had.

The other pond urchins slithered up to inspect
Alice and her exploited bottom.
For they shared the frog's lechery, although not his taste.
The lizard hissed, "My she looks like a sleeping princess
with her dainties quite undone."
And the turtle, "Gee, Gee, what a box, what a precious
slender box."
And the goldfish bubbled anxiously about giving her first aid
which the turtle was already beginning to do, somewhat pervertedl

Just then, Alice sat up yawning,
in the scampering retreat of the pondlings.
She looked about dreamily and pulled up her silkies.
"What a beautiful day," she said, as she picked up
the fumbling turtle
and placed it back in her lap,
leaning onto the cool grass,
to maybe catch another snatch of sleep
before her vicious mother called her home.

II ZEN AND TONIC

ZEN AND TONIC

Back when I was a Buddhist
I knew how to release a hypothetical duck
from an imaginary bottle without breaking
either. I knew other things I'm sure
but the duck in the bottle is crisp
and exact.
The trick was that since both duck and bottle
were imaginary, there was no problem, thus
no need for a solution. That made sense.

But the duck was still in the bottle,
trembling, trying to quack free.
I couldn't break the bottle (that was
the rule) and I couldn't kill the duck.
Back then it was as easy as saying,
"Behold, I've done it." And the roshi
would smile indulgently.
But now I've got to write it all out.
And as the duck's head squeezes free
and his fat body is gliding out,
all I hear is the sound of one hand writing
and a bottle breaking.

GRAVE ROBBING

My bones click
like tumblers when I'm still.
Some slight misalignment falls back
into place. And this vault
I'm trapped in sighs.

But I say no.
I won't be burgled by drowsiness.
I twirl my lock. Confuse the sequence.
I don't want my bolt thrown yet
not even into you.

There must be other choices
than making love or sleep.
But we don't know them, so we lock again.
Looking for new combinations.
Robbing the grave another half hour.

WAKING, THE LOVE POEM SIGHS

I make myself wake early
In a rising light
So I can roll up on an elbow
To study you.
To get that image, that raw
Romantic thrill
The nucleus of the love poem
You claim I can not write,
The poem that has haunted me for
Years clogs like a plug in
Whatever canal feeds the firey words
To my sub-vocalizing mind.

I am looking at you, full of waking
Wonder—ready to surprise you.
But nothing happens, except
A bird has awakened and the cat
Is home from stalking and looking
In the window at me. And you,
You breathe a sigh like you knew
I couldn't do it. That I could
Never wake early enough to pull the
Words out of this dream and make
Them work for me in daylight.

STEPS

"Don't step *on* anything
you can step over," my father said
as we hiked, hunting beer cans to shoot
off stumps, or sink in the river.
He learned that in the army. He was
a mine sweeper.

                    I barge
back into my mind, disobeying him.
Stepping on everything.
It is that snow filled country road, Germany.
I am the officer who drove past my father
across the unswept snow.
My jeep explodes, I explode a second time.

I trip
all the concealed wires,
whistle American tunes, jingle change in
my pockets. I give myself
away, point blank, over
and over again. Wild to meet the enemy.
I rifle through his war stories, his maxims,
crumbling them like cookies,
leaving a trail anyone could follow.

KING KONG

The white actress from America
a blondie, wearing increasingly torn and revealing clothes,
was lashed Jesus-like between two poles,
as King Kong rolled his eyes with lust,
and beat his nut-shell armored chest.
And through all his hair you could see
he was enjoying himself and his immense stay on Earth.

Reaching down, puzzled, as if about to feel his first breast,
Kong cupped up the screaming, fainting Hollywood virgin,
her lipstick intact, her hard knotted curls bouncing wildly.

And Kong, frustrated by the disproportion
of their organs
and her lush beauty
gave her an angry rattle, jerking her unconscious.
And then afraid himself, he petted her.
like an old bum might stroke his last cigar butt.

When her boyfriend, the first mate, finally came
scambling over mountains, firing his impotent forty-five,
she awoke and twisted irresistibly.
The mate squirming to have just a part of her
caught so well and struggling.
The jungle squealed and screeched and opened Kong a path
trampling deeper. Vultures separated from tree tops
and floated after them.

Kong allowed himself to be trapped,
caged,

sent to New York City.
And he scanned the crowds incessantly
slowly inferring that he had no hope of finding
a body that could sustain his.
He twisted free,
roamed the city,
saw the Empire State
and climbed it.

As the airplanes attacked him, he beat proudly
at that chest that only one would ever heave beneath
and plunged, Icarus Kong, spread eagling toward the miniature
streets.
An erection rising slowly, hopefully,
from the front of his hugh, boyish, wooly body.

You know it's coming
into your throat

It stings like food
going the wrong way

It is a round cherry
with skin so slight
a gulp will split it open

You lift it while
the wind rattles while a
moth battles at the screen

You draw it out of
your throat onto your
palate and you slide
it onto your tongue
like a beautiful cyanide
pill, a tissue keeps
its color away

And you look up now around
the ordinary room aching
like a perched cliff diver
and gnash it into stinging
song

SHORT LIVED PHENOMENA

The jasmine candies
the alleyway air and I hear a clack
of shell and asphalt in front of me.
It is the crabs tapping from the bay
across the crunch of street into yards,
into patios. Bedrooms. For three days
they come and then nothing.
Next it will be the tangle
of black lovemaking insects that glue
windshields gum radiators and
blacken the afternoons of two weeks in
August.
Then the catfish with legs
climb out of canals to stop buses,

and the snails that lick paint off
houses and cars and mailboxes. And
the new termites that three days each
June eat cupfuls of cement here and
there and die.
The Gulf slickens and bleeds,
killing its tons. The stinking hills
of beached fish for four weeks in summer
pull in the sharks.
Across my shoe a crab flops
trundling toward my house, where she is
reading.
He knows the way.

THE ORIGINAL YAWN

In the dentist office
            I am next.
I can't clamp back a
            revealing yawn.

As perhaps the original man
in his ruff jacket and fossiled face
rolled off his original woman
            and yawned.
            And she yawned.
And all the men sitting around the dawn
yawned
and rolled over to sleep.

And it has been going around since
like a dirty joke
            that everyone hears and laughs to
until eventually it is expurgated and
published in Readers Digest
where I read it
            and yawn.
And everyone in the dentist's office
            watches me
            and yawns.

RAISING MY CONSCIOUSNESS WITH HOT MUSTARD

I eat hot mustard with a spoon.
And my tongue bathes in its own juices
when I only think of horseradish.
Fire, I have to be fire in these
moments we are dressed and in separate
rooms. I torture my wet dead tongue
with green peppers and Tabasco,
mild as milk compared to the
intricate canals of your ears,
the down on your cheek, the pungent
sweat from your shoulder.
You, you are curry without wine,
you are a dozen radishes when you smile.
And when you tell me what a fool I am
for thinking of you in terms of food
(something to be merely consumed and excreted)
I see I've not made it clear enough.
Your fingers are laced with pepper-
mint when they tighten. And your
mouth seeking mine seeking yours
is the history of men and women
sharing spring water on blazing desert marches.

HELLO

Hello.
I'm not
at home. This is
a recorded voice. My voice,
the way my body flaps and trembles
through the electronic goo between us.
I want you to understand this: this message
is spoken only to evoke your response. It carries
no meaning. It is a baby strangled with a sock.
It is a ceaseless dog barking next door. It means
nothing. It is your face flattening against
the dashboard. It is your thumb sliced to
the joint, the bone pulled free.
Only so many disorganized noises
which spike our hearts, wrench
the beaks from pet canaries.
Would you please say what
is on your mind, when I
hatchet this frog's
head free. You can
speak at the croak.
Think hard now.
Your response
is being re-
corded. None
of this is
ever planned.
You have
only one
chance.
Make it
good.
Croak.

III THE LADY FROM THE DARK GREEN HILLS

LIVE STUDIO WRESTLING

The Murfreesboro Mauler peels
John Blank out of the ropes, where
he threw him,
and body slams him.
They ride together on the mat
like that for several minutes,
flipping like fish, the Mauler
grinding salt into John Blank's eyes.

They struggle to their feet
like rapist and rapee, Blank blinking
and blanching, The Mauler, mauling.
When a huge man from the studio audience
with sinking ships on his forearms
pops a packet of ketchup in his mouth
and leaps into the ring,
appalling the Mauler and drawing applause.
He goes for the villain

who steps aside neatly and plants a fist
in the ostensible tourist's throat.
The ketchup breaks open,
the fans at home slap their knees,
and the announcer stumbles on the word *hemorrhaging.*
The camera spins around, simulating chaos.
And for a second we glimpse
a policeman lighting his cigarette
and a ten year old boy dragging
his bawling brother back from the bathroom.

BARBERS, CAB DRIVERS, ZEN AND MORE

Everyone knows that no one
considers poets particularly useful
and no one encourages their son to
become one because what do they know
about making toast or selling cars
and then they ask you in the barber chair
what you do for a living and you go on
and tell them and they don't act surprised
but ask you to quote something you've written
to see if they've ever heard it, so you
freeze and melt and say something about
how your poems aren't that kind or you haven't
been writing very long, just like the time the
cab driver picked you up after a zen session
and he was the first person you'd talked to
aside from the master in almost a week
and he asks you what kind of nuts are those
guys in the robes and bald heads and you
tell him how to make french toast supreme
and how to sell a cadillac to a man on
welfare and you go on and on making him
wiser and wiser all the way to the airport,
all the way to the sideburns.

THE MUMMY

The best of us return
from death.
Boris Karloff as The Mummy,
Jesus as the Son of God.

For one thing, you didn't see
Boris hurrying anywhere.
And he didn't get angry
but held his madness in and
breathed it,
the light playing on his face
as if he stood before a burning city.

Boris knew what being dead
for 3,240 years does to someone.
And he showed it in his grace, his
positive impoliteness, his
unequivocable silences.
When others scattered, or at best
cowered, Boris merely stood,
letting the holocausts roll through him.
While others loved in leaps and fidgets
Boris loved eternal, dark,
deeply.

You could not joke with Boris.
He found things unfathomably funnier
than that.
And you couldn't pass the time of day

with him. He would stand unfocused,
taller than your voice, and might
walk away mid-sentence.

But as usual,
his power was his weakness.
His concentration was so keen
that he ignored them
as they sunk the sacred dagger wrist deep
into him.
And his eyes looked out at a distant
familiar detour, while his mummy body
withered and split open like a milkweed pod
scattering thirty centuries across the floor.

Death sweeping across him
like the wind reshaping the Sahara.

NEIMAN MARCUS

He greets me. Clothes
pruned like tight lawns
demonstrating his body,
and he suggests I leave
nothing unlooked at.
Mirrors everywhere
show us together, a thin
instrument smiling above
me in my lumpy clothes.

"Tell me how I can look that way."
"This way
sir, and what size are you?"
"I want to be your size," I say.
"Not today,
not in your color,
not in Neiman Marcus, sir.
Come back
to see us,
though."

He makes a slit in the air
between us, a perfect
perforation through which he slides,
leaving me in the glass elevator
with a twin of his, who hugs three lumpy
bags of perfect clothes.
"Nice bags," I say.
He thinks I'm not beside him.

ICE AGE TRANSLATION

I am down
the black slant of night
wet slick floor
slippery as reindeer slime.

My candle lashes
on the wall the horse
I have drawn.
The candle makes him trot.

Inside the horse
round moon marks
jounce and above the
bouncing horse are my hands
where I have outlined them
on the ice flat stone.

Horse of meat
hands of meat
moon of meat.
All run in the whipping light.

My hands move above
it again. As they did
when I first made the horse
by cracking stones.

The wick dies.
And this running horse leaves
the wall.
And is in the dark with me.
It is my secret.
No one knows yet what
miracles can be done.

TEACHING THEM TO SHOW IT

Hit the mallet on the board
and the weight rises to sting the
carnival bell.

I tell them, God is the bell,
Truth is the ding at the top.
Beauty, Death, all of it, ding!

The way to make the bell ding in
my mind is to show me the crack the
mallet makes denting the trigger board.

Show me that.
Show, don't tell me ding.

They sense this is a sideshow, poetry.
While in the main tent
jumping through fire hoops and
making lions growl at empty chairs
are Beauty and Danger and Despair.

It is a lesson I didn't intend.
That people don't pay their dollars
to hear the slow woosh of the empty trapeze.
But to see Death Defied.
They pay to look up, to creak their necks.

To see the strong man's bell fail
to ring and his blonde date rip the bell apart.

No one listens for the mallet's crack
except God-ding! And makers of God.

THE DENTIST CHAIR DREAM: THE MAN WHO ATE HIMSELF

Back into his mouth,
beyond his nutcrackers, ice breakers,
darker in than his thick carrot snappers,
surfacing like sharp-set sharks,
his wisdom teeth glared through.

He tickled himself with this new pain,
then slowly,
faster and faster he began to eat himself.
Uppers shredding away lowers,
lowers biting at uppers.
Gradually eating up into his skull
down into his neck
into his sternum.

His mouth, like a pair of red socks
rolled inside out around itself,
spread back, deliberately enclosing his pain-grated body.
Until all that remained was a strand of sun-touched hair,
and on the other end, a toe.
And then that was gone.

And what was left of him
sat up,
hearing his wisdom teeth clinking together like surgical tools,
at last unobstructed
by the rest of his body.

LUCKILY

Luckily, I'm not
a plant. I can survive
air conditioning, total shade,
or too much to drink.
My sex life
doesn't depend on wind or bees.

And I don't have ordinary roots.
I can sprout in parking lots,
send out runners in shopping malls.
The threads can scrawl out
my fingers anywhere, and I am
fastened temporarily in high winds
or thick heat,
and may bloom at any moment.

ALONE TOGETHER

The dance wears on. Sometimes we
sit. I order you a drink I know
you like. You like it.

I find the rhythm we've found
so rewarding and we are rewarded.

We dance in chairs scribbling
poems and scratching out, looking
up words in the same Thesauraus.

You cut my hair. I trim yours.
I kiss your lips. Your lips respond.
My brain is white blood instantly.

We go to bed and wake up writing
poems about each other.

There are a dozen flashing people
in the room or only two, no matter,
we know how to be alone together.

THE WINDOW: NASHVILLE TENNESSEE

Before the highways were hung overhead
we drove through the fringes of the slum, on
our way for a day in the city.

My father pointed to a shack attached
to a grocery, where black boys stood
noticing me through inches of conditioned air.
He said,
"That's where he died. See his shadow
on the window."
There was no shadow there for me,

until several Saturdays later
he reminded us to look for it.
Mother told him that he sure repeated
the same stories a lot.
Then I saw it.
The shadow of an old man
who'd sat for thirty years next to the window.
And who died months before he was noticed.
The shadow's explanation was
that getting his soul out of the room
God had scorched the window.
My brother suggested that it was like his
brownie box camera. The sun had got so used
to stopping where the old man started
that the pane was like film. His shadow
was a positive negative.
Then my mother offered
that the story'd been made to suit the window.
My father looked at her.
My brother went on with his box camera theory.
And I stared and stared
at the film in my head
that was to hold that image regardless.

THE LADY FROM THE DARK GREEN HILLS: A LEGEND

she came flying out of the dark green mountains
behind four thousand cubic centimeters
and seven feet of black shining steel
no top   with her hair four feet flying in her dust
and her face locked in a bloodless grin   with goggles

she knocked the props out of the village security
as her roar whined away in a flurry of gravel
and everyone
everyone knew she was on the prowl

some said it was courting
for she always came at the softest part of day
and her hundred wounded jaguars howled through the dusk
toward something

the children at their games   on lawns   over the road
would stop   and weakly watch her pass
babies wailed   mothers clenched their faces
and fathers remembered their youthful wish:
to sit beside the black governess from the dark green hills
and bite the evening's neck with her

and the older boys stayed up scared all night
to maybe catch her on a slow return
but each dawn   she tore past the milkman   shied his horse
squealing up through the hairpins toward her lair
the dust hanging till eleven some mornings
as a warning not to follow

but as they don't finish telling in,
"the world stands aside for someone who knows where he's
going"
'there's part of the world that gets sucked along in the wash'
for weren't there three of the biggest and most reckless
of the village boys who primed a '34 Ford all summer

just to race the panther back home
and didn't they tear through the dusty dawn after her
pinned to their seats in fright and speed
and didn't only one of them come back   half crazy
with talk of a castle of coal
and live jaguars, chained to trees

and didn't they almost get a search party
to hunt for the other two
until one of the orphaned mothers dreamed
that the black vampiress had told her to forbid the search
and now when only mr. arthur and ben barrows
remember having seen her when they were children
wasn't there a reporter here to find out the details
of the legend
didn't ben refuse to say anything
and didn't mr. arthur die a week after the young man left

and then   didn't a strange little lady   as white as death
with yellow rouge and jet black hair
come out of the dark green mountains
in a long black sports car
and leave it for a tune up
and didn't bedlow the mechanic disappear mysteriously
soon after

and didn't the legend settle down
and get paved under
as the village grew slowly
into a town

Books of Poetry from Three Rivers Press

Chapbooks

Uccello's Horse, Richard R. O'Keefe (1972)
The Dancer's Step, Ann Hayes (1973)
By Breathing In and Out, Albert Drake (1974)
The Obedience School, Greg Kuzma (1974)
Election, William L. Fox (1974)
Tonight is the Night of the Prom, Mark Jarman (1974)

Full Length Collections

Petroglyphs, Sam Hamill (1975)
The Lady From The Dark Green Hills, Jim Hall (1976)